Incipient

COLLECTION OF POETRY

I

1977–1982

Rosa M. Diaz

Incipient
Collection of Poetry I
1977–1982

Copyright © 2021 by Rosa M. Diaz.

Paperback ISBN: 978-1-63812-067-4
Ebook ISBN: 978-1-63812-068-1

All rights reserved. No part in this book may be produced and transmitted in any form or by any means, electronic, or mechanical, including photocopying, recording, or by any information storage and retrieval system, without permission in writing from the copyright owner.

The views expressed in this work are solely those of the author and do not necessarily reflect the views of the publisher hereby disclaims any responsibility for them.

Published by Pen Culture Solutions   07/19/2021

Pen Culture Solutions
1-888-727-7204 (USA)
1-800-950-458 (Australia)
support@penculturesolutions.com

To my family
For their support,
To my friends
For their words,
To my son
For his encouragement.

Introduction

I was born in Mexico City in 1963. I am the sixth child of eight children. We lived in Mexico City until 1968. I was just about to turn five when we moved to Ciudad Morelos, a small town in the desert of Baja California, near the US border. We lived there four years and those years transformed my life in many ways.

In January of 1973, I reunited with my family who had already emigrated to the California Central Valley. We live in the small town of Atwater the first year. Then we moved to the countryside where we lived four years. Finally, in 1978 we moved to our own home in Winton.

Because of my studies and as an adult, I lived in Turlock for six years during the 1980s.

My only child was born in 1991 and now, he and I, moved to Modesto in 2000.

I attended Mitchell Elementary School 1973-1976

Mitchell Sr. Junior High School 1976-1978

Atwater High School 1978-1982

Merced College 1982-1984

California State University, Stanislaus, where I graduated in 1990.

I started writing when I was 13 or 14 years old. I began writing in Spanish, my native language. It took me a few years to be confident enough and inspired to start writing in English, but even then, I always had the idea and the basics in Spanish. Many more years later, I began translating my own work to both languages because I know that so much of the content is lost in the translation and nobody knows better than me what I want to communicate.

Unfortunately, I threw away many of my first poems, without thinking about tomorrow. Also, out of malice or I do not know what, some people kept or lost some of my writings when I let them read what I had. And to top it off, over the years and through technology, I lost other poems and short stories. And still today, I see that every written thing is so important and every loss hurts to the deepest.

I remember that my best friend was self-appointed secretary. It started as something short, simplistic, and more than anything, it was for fun of the rhyme. She wrote down whatever I told her when the inspiration hit. She had a legible writing and I had the ideas, prompt and continuous.

Little by little, I started writing about my views and feelings with the limitations as a sheltered child. Note, when I speak of love, I speak of emotional love, not physical love.

If I could go back in time, I would write about my friends and people I saw every day, so many stories, so many incidents, so many experiences lived but never recorded. I would strongly write of what I see and opine and not what is personal or what I feel. I would focus on social problems and issues dealing with youth, points of view that go with my age. I would leave aside fantasyland, and issues I do not know about and what I have not experienced. If I could go back in time, I would write differently and not try to be someone I was not. But those errors opened my appetite for writing, observation and to the subconscious.

In my childhood, I had a group of friends in school. We were at the same level mentally, socially, family and economically. It was laughter and conversations with no end but, one on one, the conversations turned serious and personal. They trusted me with their personal and family problems. Those friendships lasted through my childhood until I graduated from high school. Therefore, I must also admit that, at times, I appropriated the feelings, the points of view, the incidents and the problems of other people that inspired me to write.

Thanks to all the people who have come into my life, directly or indirectly, because that has strengthened my life. I have learned a lot from all of them and every action and word has made me who I am. Thank you.

In this book, all the poems were originally written in Spanish.

Contents

SPIRITUALITY 1

Delirium 3
My God 4
Guadalupe 5
Lord 6
Thankful 7
Join Me 8

INCIPIENT 9

Studying 11
For Me 13
I Depart Happy 14
The Poet 15
When You Return 17
Desolation 18
Mad World 19
Earth Friend 21
Frustration 23
My Treasure 24

YOUNG LOVE 25

Rumors 27
I Believe 28
Love 29
Everything 30
First Love 31
Didn't Let Me Love You..32
Thinking Of You 33
Distance 34
I Apologize 35
Go Away 36
Dismissal 37
When You Leave 38
You Well Know 39
Come Back 40
Give Me A Kiss 41
Memories 42
I Miss You 43
Tears For A Memory 44
Your Departure 45
You Leave Me 46
Tell Me 47
Wishes 48
Do Not Make Me Suffer 49
Your Eyes 50
You Belong To Another 51
This Day 52

ILLUSIONS 53

Fantasies 55
Farewell 56
Loneliness 57
My Dreams 58
Fantasy Drawings 59

Intimacy 60
A Couple 61
Love Letters 62
Dreams 63
Different 64
Hopes 65
If You Were 66
Love In An Interval 67
I Am Sorry 68
Our Love 69
I Need You 70
Forever An Illusion 71
Where Are You? 72
Nostalgia 73
Doubt 74
My Pleading 75
My Love For You 76
The Day 77
Tomorrow 78

EVENTS 79

A Father 81
That Party 82
Essence Of Innocence 83
Mother's Day 86
St. Nick 87
Fifteen Years 88
February 14 89
Our Day 90
Sweet Sixteen 91
Amid Smoke And Ashes 92

SURROUNDINGS 93

Springtime 95
Flowers Of My Garden 96
A Withered Rose 97
Under The Rain 98
Shelter 99
Moon 100
A Bird 101
Roses 102
Autumn Sentiments 103
Bird In Freedom 104

REMEMBRANCE 105

Yearning 107
Cinco De Mayo 109
My Homeland 110

REFLECTIONS 111

Life And Death 113
Final Loss 114
I Am Nothing 115
Youth 116
Craziness 117
Tears, Tears 119
Lamentations 120
Time 121
Lies 122
A Vagabond 123
Time Goes By 124
My Luck 125
Aspiration 126

DEDICATIONS 127

Your Voice 129
My Friend 130
You 131
Greetings 132
To My Mother 133
Graduation 134

SPIRITUALITY

I turn to the heavens
When I am joyful
Or hurt.
I turn to the heavens
And render
My gratitude
Often
For the things I have
And the life I breathe.
The Master King
Is always
Close to me.

Delirium

I hear the thunders
In a Holy Saturday.

It is the rain
And the tears
Of God
From the infamies
Of the world,
It is the weeping
Of the souls
Who are in hell
For the torture
They cannot stand,
It is also
The sad cry
For the overwhelming
Loneliness
Around those in heaven.

Their wailing
Converted
Into thunder,
Is constant.
The day turned gloomy,
It rains and rains
With no end,
God
Has no mercy on us.

Silence!
The wailing from God
Is delirious.

He asks for peace,
Tolerance
And compassion
For the neighbor
And servitude
Only to Him.
He offers us
Eternal life
And the world
Responds
With false promises
Of behaving well
And caring for others.

The rave on earth.
Is fretful.
As death is felt,
People ask
For peace and mercy.
They sob and moan,
They join a church
And believe
Heaven is earned
And their soul is clean
By asking
For forgiveness,
Though their lives
Were of amusement,
Evil and selfishness
And their actions
Were nothing pleasant.

April 7, 1980

My God

My Lord,
I do not ask for glory
Or condemnation.
I simply ask you
To take me away
Where you believe
Is best for me.

I put myself
In your hands.
Do not let me fall
Onto temptation,
Do not let me fall
In hopelessness.
Protect me from the hell
Where I am now.
I do not ask for heaven,
I do not deserve it
But take me away
Where they need me
And not have me
Out of obligations.

Give me kindness
To treat others.
Clean my heart
Of ill feelings
To give you my soul
Clean and loving.
Give me enough days
To fulfill my wishes.
Give me a tomorrow
Of hope
As reason for living.

Guide me
On the good path
So that I may deserve
To be by your side.
Do not let me think
Of vengeance.
Help me be forgiving
To everyone.
Do not let me be
Cruel or selfish,
And do not blind me
To reality.
Do not let me
Fill my soul
With lies and deceit.

I implore you—
Be merciful
So I will be with others.
Let me know
I am not forgotten.
Give me hope
To stay alive.

My God, forgive me
For thinking of death,
But it is a relief
For my sorrows
And luck.
Protect me, to be better.

February 4, 1980

Guadalupe

To our brunette Lady,
Queen of my house,
I come to say
In this modest poem,
I am bound to you
For this joy
And suffering
I give and felt.

At your shrine
I come to kneel.
I come
To give my soul.
Though it lives
In sin,
It recovers
With your guidance.

Lady of Guadalupe,
You, who are there,
In the highness
Of heaven,
Give me your blessings,
And forgive me
For not following
The path
Of your words.

Our beloved Lady,
My song
Is for you.
Never forget those
Suffering
With no guidance.
Send your mercy
And look down below,
For we are nothing
Without you.

November 24, 1979

Lord

I know
I am not alone.
I could be
In the desert
All alone
And I would feel
Your guidance
And imagine
Your presence
Before me.

You help me
Continue in life.
You heal my sorrows,
With Your blessing,
My weakness
Is strength.

The difficult
Problems
Are easier
When you are near.
In my frustrations,
When I feel
The most depressed,
I feel your hand
Over me
And I regain
The lost faith.

Before you
I have no pride
Or sorrows
Because you are
My witness
And you are
In my conscience.
You are
The eternal promise
For which I have to live.

May 4, 1982

Thankful

I give thanks to life,
It has given me so much,
Although I deserve nothing,
And what I complain about.

I give thanks to God
For giving me life,
Though it is what it is,
Though I suffer
And enjoy,
I feel life in me.

Thanks to my parents
For giving me life
And my being,
To my friends
Who understood me,
Thanks for all
They offered me
And for their truth.

I do not know
Whom to thank
For this quiet
Expression
But I am truly thankful
For the words
That come out of me.
Thankful
For the knowledge
I have acquired,
And for having what I have.

I thank
Those around me
Today and tomorrow
So it will be.

March 24, 1980

Join Me

Join my hand
To share
My support
And give you
The love
That you need,
Join my soul
To bring you
Encouragement
And the comfort
Of life.

Join my hand,
My friend,
My brother,
And together
Walk
Towards love,
Join my hand
And let us forget
The sorrows
And pain.

Join my voice
And let us laugh
Hard and loud,
Join my soul
To give you
What no one
Has given you before.

Join my hand
To help
Those who suffer
With loyalty
And respect,
Showing hope
And understanding,
Join my hand
And together
Make
Of this revolution,
A world of love,
Join my soul
And pray
For eternal peace.

December 10, 1980

INCIPIENT

Incipient I am,
A novice
In the art
Of the letters,
Transmitted
In the simplicity
Of the experiences.
Incipient,
Always an apprentice,
Of what others
Teach me.

Incipient I am,
In meditation
And self-analysis
On what I have lived.
Incipient
In understanding
Where the emotional
Root is
And where it comes from.

Studying

By studying,
I learned
To give and receive.
I also learned
Not to lie
And of course,
To search
For the truth.

They taught me
To read
And to write
From *a*
To infinity.
I learned
Of numbers,
Of letters
And syllables,
Of easy words,
And short rhymes.

In school,
Everything
Was fun
With my friends.
What I learned,
I, later, taught it.
To them.

Studying,
I learned
Of foreign tongues.
I learned
To talk,
To express myself.
And with my studying,
I speak better.
I learned
Of homework
And, in compositions,
I wrote
Of my feelings
And views
In whichever language
It was.

In the books
Of history,
Science,
English,
And math
I wrote
My memories
In simple verses
From left to right.
In my art,
Singing
And dancing classes,
With my imagination
Flying freely,
Everything
Was more interesting.

They gave me
Pencils,
Books,
And binders,
But instead
Of writing
My homework,
I would write names
And draw faces,
Things
And silly stuff.

In school,
When studying,
In my classes,
When speaking
And from the books,
I have learned a lot
About letters
And numbers
And deep sentiments.

May 11, 1979

For Me

You are like the roses,
Soft and beautiful.

You are like the flowers,
Pure
With no sorrows.

You are like the angels,
And like carnations.

You are like the night,
Where there are no regrets.

You are naïve,
Like kindness
And sweet like happiness.

You are like the spark
Of two hearts
And fiery like passion.

In winter, I feel cold,
In summer, I feel hot,
I do not know what I would do
If I did not have your love.

December 12, 1977

I Depart Happy

If I arrived
In this world
Only to suffer,
I depart from it happy.

I have not found
A true love
To give me warmth
When I need it most.
Everything
Takes me to the abyss
If I do not have a friend.

February 27, 1978

The Poet

The poet
Writes down
His imagery,
His thoughts,
And his own
And others' feelings.
The poet
Interprets
His sorrows
And joys
And presents them
In written words.
The poet plays
With the words
Learned.

The poet
Is who hears
The heart
And not
The reasoning.
The poet
Customizes
All possible
Emotions.

The poet
Is a sentimental person
Seeking
A quiet place
To write his ideas.
He describes
His efforts
Under the moon
And stars
And sees the sun rise
On a new day.

The poet
Writes the events
In rhymes
And verses.
He has within
Letters
And rhythms,
And after writing,
He is free
Of his burden.

The poet
Is one
Who expresses
His opinions
Against
And in favor
Of the world
In a subtle manner.
The poet
Writes
Of the anguish
And distress
Of love
And loneliness.

The poet
Writes of
And describes
The exterior.

He is spontaneous,
He is who writes
What is forbidden,
And private,
What is secretive—
And from the heart.

The writers
Learn to listen,
See and be silent.
They observe
And analyze,
Plan and polish.
They appropriate
Others' feelings
And opinions
But, if honest,
Give their credit.

I say
What a poet is
Simply because
This is how I am.
But not every poet
Can be considered
To be like this.
What I say,
I say because of me.

September 5, 1979

When You Return

My heart is yours.
That is my illusion.

I love you.
When I first saw you,
I fell in love with you.

You were my first love.
With your kisses
I had the warmth
That I yearned for
And needed.

Now you are leaving,
It is the worst thing
For me.
When we were together,
It was all smiles.
You will miss me,
And I know
You will return.

It will be like before,
Like in my dreams.
It will be happiness
In my heart and soul.

December 5, 1977

Desolation

All my hopes
Have vanished,
My eyes
Are teary,
And the skies
Are rainy.
So often, I prayed
For God
To help me
And improve
My luck,
But my efforts
Have failed.

Failures,
I have had many
But even so,
I am not defeated.
Unhappy I am,
It is exposed
When I write
And I am happy
When I talk,
Advice and guide.
It is
What people say
But they do not see
What is in front
Of them.

I suffer
Disappointments
About work
And love.
What's life for,
If everything
I touch
Is destroyed,
And if everyone
I love
Is gone,
Leaving me
Empty handed
And a confused
Heart.

May 10, 1980

Mad World

The world
Is mad.
We are all mad
As we are here
Destroying ourselves.
Instead of loving
One another,
We are against
Others,
For no reason.

The rich
Throw away
Money and food,
And others die
In misery
For lack
Of water and bread.
The rich
Won't notice
The poor,
The old embrace
Their solitude,
The sick
Feel rejected,
The innocent child
Is abused
And women
Are demoralized.
Men take advantage
Of their strength
And exceed
In their power
Practicing
Their vile customs.
From this
No one emerges
A winner.

Mad world
We are.
We laugh
At others' pain,
And we own it
For our satisfaction.
We are selfish,
We have no respect
Or pity.
Grudges, hate,
And vengeance
Fill the mind
With malevolence.

Where is God
Hiding?
Doesn't he see
How people
Suffer more
Than they enjoy?
So many people
Need parents,
Friends, children.
Others need security
And trust
In themselves.
Where is God?
Doesn't he see
The depression,

Anguish
And melancholy
Fill the soul
And empty the mind
Of dreams?

God,
Where are you?
Where do you hide?
Don't you see
We need you
Here and now?

So many of us
Want to love
And follow
The teachings
Of our Creator,
But it is easier
To act out
The opposite.
This is not right,
We have to think
Of the future
Of what may come
But temptation
Is great
And the provocation
Is there.

I will pray
To the Creator
To lift our penance.
I pray
He hears
My pleading
That I say each night:
God,
Watch over us.
Watch over this world.
Though we are sinners,
We all are your children.
We need you
And deserve
Your guidance.

October 10, 1979

Earth Friend

Earth friend,
You are making
Of this world
A disaster.
You do not know me,
I come
From the moon
To give you
Some good fortune.

I live
Among the stars
And planets
In the immense
Infinite.
Here, you change
Everything,
But there
Things remain
The same.

Earth friend,
You kill
Your brother
And destroy
Your surroundings
For material
Things.
You do not see
The damage
You cause
And do.

You think
You are happy,
But no—you are not.
Everyone cries
Around you.
Poor wretch!

I pity you.
You are the thorn
Instead of the petal.
The divine
Beauty
Is worthless
In your eyes
Until you feel lost.

Earth friend,
I am not a ghost,
Neither am I real,
But to the soul,
I am loyal.
You are not
Like this,
Poor wretch.
You are evil,
You are at war
With no end.
You could
Have been eternal,
But you
Have destroyed
The world.
Today,
Nothing is left
Of your past.

Earth friend,
In the beginning
You were ignorant,
But now
You are a disgrace.
You were an angel
In infancy
But now,
As if possessed,
You commit
All sorts of evil
With ease
And do not see
Your personal value.

You travel
And explore
To find yourself,
And now
You want to come
To my house
Just to dirty it
As if it was yours.

I see you
From above
And do not wish
To be like you.
Looking at me,
You get scared,
But it should be
The other way
Around,
Watching
What you do
Day by day.

I am happy
As I am,
I would give
Nothing
To be like you.

October 20, 1980

Frustration

I feel frustrated,
I want peace,
I have come to the point
Of saying
And thinking
That if I had my wish,
My spiritual peace
Would be
Much different.

I, gladly
And peacefully,
Offer my body
And soul
To God
And the world,
Knowing
That my departure
Would bring peace
And happiness.

To the world,
I do not show
The anguish
I feel
With my tears
Or whimpering
But with my actions
And what I think.

Because of
My frustration,
I wish to be
The only one
On earth
Going through this
So others may enjoy
The benefits
Of another life.

December 8, 1980

My Treasure

I have a treasure,
Big and valuable.
No, it is not gold
Or silver
Or any material thing.

The treasure
I have
Is neither coins
Nor a loved one.
It is simply
My feelings,
My thoughts
And my words.

My treasure
Is only mine.
No one can ever
Take it away,
Because my treasure
Is my imagination.

God has given me
The strength to live
And the qualities
To be different.
It may not be
All right,
But the treasure I have
Is to express
What I feel
And to write

My thoughts
About myself
And the whole world.

No one is perfect,
And I should not
Complain,
Because I am
Neither less
Nor better
But I do realize
The treasure I have.

I know
We all have
Some hidden
Valuable quality
That, for fear
Or shame,
We do not show
But I,
In written words,
Stated my feelings.

My treasure
Is individual,
And if anyone tries,
They cannot steal it,
Because it's in me,
And my knowledge
Of expression.

August 22, 1979

YOUNG LOVE

Crushes come
By a smile,
A glance,
A word,
Some walk away
Hastily
In search of their goal,
Some pass by
Unnoticed
As friendly souls,
But others,
Settle down
And remain stagnant
In the soul
And memories.

Rumors

They say you love me,
I do not know
What to think.
They are just rumors
Spread by their speech.

Do not be put off
For something
Unimportant,
If it's true,
Quickly
They will make me
Know,
And then
Revenge will follow.

Rumors circulate
About me,
And that is why
You changed.
In the end,
Everyone
Is just the same:
They do not respect
The feelings
Of others.

If I knew
What they have said
About me,
I am sure
I could
Make you change
Just by saying
That you
Make me happy.

October 6, 1978

I Believe

I believe
I am falling for you.

I believe everything
Would be happiness
But without you
It would crumble.

I believe I love you
But because of others
We cannot be happy
Because of rumors
They only invent.

I believe
I was not lucky
With you.
They did not let me
Love you
And so I believe
It is better for me to leave.

October 5, 1978

Love

Love, I feel for you,
Hoping you feel
The same for me.

A rose bouquet
Is beautiful and silky,
Proof of true love.

I love you
But I cannot say it
But I know you love me
And we feel
The same way.

Between us
There is so much love
As I had always wished.
Thank you,
My love
For being by my side.

December 21, 1977

Everything

You are the light
To my darkness,
You are the sun
To my days,
You are the moon
To my nights,
You are the joy
To my sadness,
You are all the good
To my sinfulness.

You are the dream
To my reality,
You are the love
To hate,
You are the smile
To my tears,
You are the flower
In my garden,
You are the truth
To my lies,
You are
Beautiful poetry.

You are
My forever dream,
You are
A special craziness,
And I give you
My heart
With love
And tenderness.

You are everything
And you are
Also my great love
And a true friend
Who gets all my trust
And gives me hope
Things will be better
Again.

July 7, 1979

First Love

It is said
That first love
Is only an illusion
And others say
That one's first love
Is special and true.

The first love
Is the one that teaches
And the one
We learn from.
We learn of sadness,
Happiness
And misunderstandings.

With our first love,
We learn to dream,
To smile more,
To love and yearn.

The first love
Is the one
That makes us adults
And shows us
There is so much new
That, as children,
We never thought
Could happen.

We never love again
As we love
The first time.
Although
It may be an illusion,
The first love
Will always be
Special.

May 21, 1979

Didn't Let Me Love You

They did not let me
Love you,
I say this sincerely.
They told me
I was too young.
But, what do they know
About matters
Of the heart?

When I met you,
Your eyes
Impressed me,
Green eyes,
Bewitching eyes
And I loved
The self-confidence.

I loved the idea
Of being your girl
Even if
The old-fashioned way,
But it did not happen
Because of my youth.

You left
Just saying
That you loved me,
And I thanked you.
Perhaps someday
We will meet again.

Keep in mind
That I fell in love
But they did not let me
Love you.
Still, I will keep you
In my heart forever.

May 15, 1979

Thinking Of You

I spend each night
Unable to sleep,
Thinking about you
And a thousand
Other things.

Each morning,
When the sun comes out,
I look
Through my window
And I remember
You again.

By the afternoon,
The sun
Starts to disappear,
When I remember
Your love
And your pitiful lies.

In the darkness,
I remember you sweetly,
In dreams
Of intense liberty.

You are in my mind
Of dreams
And reality.

October 9, 1978

Distance

Long is the distance
Between you and me,
But we are together
In our thoughts.
If it weren't
For the distance,
We would be together,
Body and soul.
We would be at morn.

In the distance,
We long to return
To the places, we dream.
At times, love
Is stronger
For what is no longer there.
Distance
Makes us reconsider,
Understand
And even yearn.

Distance
Can bring people closer
Or drive them
Farther apart.
Distance
Makes some people
Be forgotten,
But that is only if we let it
Happen.

June 12, 1979

I Apologize

I apologize
For coming
To bother you
But I needed to talk.
No, do not worry,
It will not happen again.
I apologize,
I could not help it
This time.

Apologies I ask.
Your love for me
Came to an end
But hear me out,
I plead.

Since you left,
I live saddened.
You killed
My dreams,
And with no regard,
You hurt me
With your rejection.

I only came
To cause pity.
Apologies. I ask
For the last time,
And then I will leave.

I apologize
If I came to bother you.
It will not happen again,
But today,
I could not help it.

October 17, 1979

Go Away

You tell me
You are leaving
With me,
Leave now,
If that is your wish.

If one day
You come back
To me,
I will welcome you.

But for now
Go away,
Feel your freedom.

You leave,
Goodbye.

June 19, 1978

Dismissal

People are strange,
At times they show
One thing
And mean another.
You showed me love
And confused
Your words
And I suffer
The consequences
Of your cruel
Indifference.

I only asked
One last favor,
To dance
To the rhythm
Of the melody
But you left
Before I said it.

It was only
A fantasy
You did not want
The same thing I did.
I was learning
To love you
And you rejected me.
I never lost hope
But today,
Though it may be
Too late,
I dismiss you.

I am happy
That you left.
You thought
I would cry,
But no,
I am not sad
And I will not start
Because of you.
My dismissal
For you
Is from now on an end.
Be happy,
For I have
Already begun.

May 21, 1980

When You Leave

Anguish
Is what I feel
When you leave,
When you are
No longer near.

Jealousy
Is what I feel
Thinking you might be
With someone else
And you may not even
Remember me.

Sadness
Is what I feel
Thinking
You might not come back
And also
How much I love you.

Impatience
Is what I feel
When you take long
To come back
And I think
It may be too late
To be together.

Tears
Are what I shed
When you tell me,
I do not love you,
And I call you a coward.

Happiness
Is what I feel
As I see you return
And open the door
To my house
And my heart.

May 6, 1979

You Well Know

You know well
I love you
But you
Do not take notice.
You know well
I dream of you
And want to be
In your game.

You know well
You are everything
To me
And that I feel
So lonesome.
I know
You love me
But you want me
To beg you.

August 16, 1979

Come Back

My dear,
I want you back,
I need you.
Just because it's so much
My sadness,
I want you back to me.

I love you
And I cannot forget you
And I want you back.
With only five words
I will express my hope:
I wish you'd come back.

Because without you
I am not happy,
I want you back to me.

June 25, 1978

Give Me A Kiss

Give me a kiss
So tenderly
That provokes
My insanity.
Give me a kiss
Where you put
Your heart
And your love.
Give me a kiss,
Not only one,
But two or three,
To let me know
You love me.

Give me a kiss,
Passionately,
And I will say
You always
Loved me.
Give me
A burning kiss
As my love
Is ever growing.
Give me a kiss
With all your feelings
In it.

Give me a kiss
Where I am
In your thoughts.
Give me
An intense kiss
With all your love.
Give me a kiss
And never leave.
I always
Want you near.

April 14, 1978

Memories

When I met you
I said hello
And now that you leave,
I say goodbye.
I will be alone
To remember
The story of us.

I will remember everything
You said to me.
I will not forget the joy
You brought me.

I will remember
I loved you
With all my heart
And I will not have
A moment of peace
Because of the farewell
You give me.

April 17, 1978

I Miss You

I miss you.
It is all my lips
Know and can say.
The hours seem like years,
And nothing
Makes me happy.

I miss you
And I cannot forget you
As I still remember
The day you left.

I wish to throw
My voice in the air
And scream aloud
That I love you,
That I miss you.

But I cannot tell anyone
That I miss you
Because they hardly listen.

May 30, 1979

Tears For A Memory

I remember
Very clearly
Our sad farewell
Although
It's in distant past.
I remember I cried,
I remember
I did not dare say,
Stay.
I am nothing
Without you.
It just crossed
My thoughts,
And I only sighed.
With a cracked voice
You told me,
Farewell, my love.

I remember
Your eyes
Clouded from the tears,
Telling me
Of your desire
To kiss me,
To hold me
In your arms,
But you did not dare
To say it.

I remember
Our farewell,
The sadden sky,
The day,
The place,
The people,
Everything
Is in my memory.
This has become
An unforgettable
Story
In my imagination.

That night
I saw myself crying
And today I feel tears
Roll down my face.
I cry for a farewell
In the past
And I feel my heart beat,
Lifeless.

June 7, 1980

Your Departure

Your figure
Vanished with the wind,
I saw you depart,
Your lips
Touched my skin
As you said goodbye.

I do not force you
To love me,
You were free
To do so.
Later today,
When the sun sets
And the light
Of the stars
And the gleaming
Of the moon
Join me,
Tenderly
I will think of you.

May that cover
The emptiness
Of the solitude
That you leave
In my heart,
Which shows with sighs
As I say goodbye.

September 15, 1982

You Leave Me

I am in love
With you,
I have confessed it
To myself
Many times.
You drive me crazy
Though
I get nothing
In return.

I wish to always
Taste on your lips
The honey of love
That you give
With urgency
In those moments
Of passion.

In the chapel
Of the town
Where I was born,
I prayed to God
To make me happy
By giving me
Your love
And your future,
But I think
It will not be.

I love you
Hopelessly,
You are my obsession
And as I see
Your silhouette
Disappear
On the horizon,
I feel inundated
With my tears.

February 26, 1980

Tell Me

Tell me,
If you do not love me,
Tell me sincerely,
I will handle
The truth,
Even if it means
Solitude
While you are filled
With joys.

Your name
Cannot come out
Of my heart,
And if it does,
It may die.

I wish
Your forgetfulness,
I wish
The transition,
But I wish more
For your affection.

January 21, 1978

Wishes

I wish to see you,
I wish to embrace you,
I wish to kiss you.

But wishes
They will remain
Because I know
You will not be back.

I wish to be with you,
It is all I ask.

I wish to see you again,
I do not care
Where, when,
Or with whom
You might be,
I simply wish
To see you again.

May 30, 1979

Do Not Make Me Suffer

You ask me to leave
And you know well
That I love you.
For you,
I would give my life,
I would give anything
I have for you.

But if you do not love me,
Tell me.
Whatever may be,
Always tell me the truth.
Tell me
If what you feel
Is friendship,
Affection or love.

I want you to be mine,
But, here, I say,
The day you do not feel
As I think you feel,
Without losing time
Tell me so,
And do not make me suffer
With your indecision.

If one day
You know
I live saddened,
Know
It is because of you
And you have
The solution.
Do not make me suffer,
I would give my life
For you.

As a favor I ask,
Do not mock
My feelings.
I am like this
Because of you,
Because I love only you.

September 30, 1979

Your Eyes

Your eyes
Are like the sea,
That let out the tears
With ease,
They are like the beyond,
Like the infinite,
The night and the stars,
They are
Like the sun
And the moon,
Like something
In time opportune.

Your eyes
Are like paradise
But indecisive.
They are like happiness
And sadness,
Like beauty
And loneliness.

Your eyes
Can be big or small,
Reflecting joy,
Pain or sorrow.

January 21, 1978

You Belong To Another

From your hand
I got a flower,
Now you belong
To another
And I feel so much pain.

If I am to forget you,
You have to leave,
Stay!
I will leave.

But being next to others,
They will lie to you easily,
And you will think of me
As I will think of you.

January 29, 1978

This Day

Today I felt
Dreams renewed
In my heart.
There are no doubts
In my soul,
Everything
Is clean and pure
For you.

Today, this day,
I have relived
All that was lost.

Today
When you leave,
I wanted to say
That I love you the most.

Today I feel your love
But I will always remember it
So I can live.

July 31, 1978

ILLUSIONS

Imagination
Runs wild
With limitations
Of a sheltered life,
Simple and innocent.
Imagination
Comes in illusions
As the product
Of what we search
And need.

Fantasies

Fantasy
Is to see
The shiny sun
In the midst
Of a thunderstorm.

Fantasy
Is to cry
From sadness
And laugh happily.

Fantasy
Is to see the night,
Moon and stars,
And then, suddenly,
The sun
And a beautiful day.

Fantasy
Is imagination
That you and I have.
It is to see
Everything
Beautiful around us.

For me
Everything is a fantasy,
A dream
Where there are no lies.

Fantasy is the life
You give me
Without asking
For something
In exchange.

March 18, 1979

Farewell

We gave each other
A kiss,
A farewell
And oblivion.
But, despite that,
I could not
Forget you.
The kiss
Is pinned
On my lips.
I carry the farewell
In my heart,
And the oblivion
I cannot remember now.

Those caresses
We shared
For the last time
And those words
We told each other
Are not easy
To forget.

When we go out
And see new faces,
We will not forget
Our love.
Not for a farewell
Or an oblivion,
We will not remember us.

To this day
I haven't forgot you—
I will not even try—
Because you are
In my mind
All the time.

July 5, 1979

Loneliness

How sad is loneliness!
If it's not the body,
It is the soul.
And loneliness
Makes life bitter.

I feel alone,
And nothing
Comforts me.
But I am not so alone
If I have your memories.
I think of the good times
We enjoyed together,
And those fill my time.

But loneliness
Is present at all times
And has no rival.
If it is true, what I hear
That loneliness
Is a disease
That is cured
With a thought
Of love,
Then may you
Never be lonesome
As I am now.

July 21, 1979

My Dreams

One morning
In March
I woke up crying
About silly things
I had dreamt about.

I dreamt
They took me away
From you
Knowing
How much I love you.
They wanted us to suffer
And keeping us apart
They tried
To make us forget
Each other.

I woke up startled.
After a while
Your words
Comforted me
And I felt loved
And protected.

September 4, 1979

Fantasy Drawings

I am left
With my dreams anew
But I offer you
My love
And my open arms.

I am being tested,
I cannot find you,
It is a mirage
That you are not
By my side,
If yesterday I felt you
And saw you
Next to me
And you were
Loving me.

I wish to draw you
In a crystal piece
For your unique beauty.
Fantasy drawings
I want to have
Of you,
Over the seas
I see you
Firm and calm,
Wise, kind
And interesting.

Your virtues come
In reflections
In front of nature
So happily.
Fantasy drawings,
I want
Of you,
To see you
Happily smiling
For being flattered.

February 25, 1981

Intimacy

Intimacy is
A man and a woman
In solitude.

Intimacy is
A dark night
When crazy things
Are done.

Intimacy is
Loving you always,
From January
To December.

Intimacy is
Making of us free.

February 25, 1978

A Couple

A man and a woman
Have thousands
Of things to do.

A man and a woman—
Doesn't matter
If they're rich or poor—
To love each other.

A man and a woman,
To love each other,
Doesn't matter their
Age, color, or religion.

A man and a woman.
It does not matter
That they are alone,
They can be understood.

A man and a woman,
Whichever way
And wherever,
Can love each other
But not forget one another.

March 31, 1978

Love Letters

Loving you so much
You left me.
My laughter
Turned into tears
And I forgot to live.

I believed you
So far away
When I received
Your letters
In which you wrote,
I love you,
I love you.
Believing
It was nonsense,
I decided
To forget about you.

So many times
I have contemplated
The infinite sky,
Mistaking nature
With poetry,
Remembering
Your words,
Your letters,
Your life and mine.

Letters and letters
I received,
In each letter you said,
I love you,
I cannot live
Without you.

I see the couples
Walk by in the rain.
They remind me
Of you and me.
I ask myself
If this rain
Are your tears
That you shed for me,
But if that's the case,
Please do not cry,
I do not deserve
So much from you.

Your letters,
Your words,
Your "I love you,"
I remember it all
And I ask myself
How it would have been
Us together.
I call them
Love letters
With no good reason.

October 17, 1980

Dreams

In dreams I feel,
In fantasies I live.
I am not a beggar,
Nor do I feel the cold
When I dream of you.

I dream
We are together,
United by love,
In paradise,
Close to God.

I feel
Like a princess
Next to you,
I believe
To be dreaming
When you kiss me
And caress me
In unsurpassed
Manners,
I dream myself
Your prisoner
Behind the bars
Of love
With the tenderness
You give.

I dream myself
Next to you
Every night,
But the awakening
Is suffering for me.

June 28, 1980

Different

Your hands ask
For a tender touch,
Your eyes ask
To be closed,
Your lips ask
To be kissed.

But I cannot love,
I have nothing
More to give,
I have
No more dreams.

It is not like before,
We are different now.
I ask you
To leave me alone
And try to forget me.

June 28, 1978

Hopes

I am poor.
I have no fortune,
The only hope
I had left
Was your love.

You wanted
To leave
To wander
Through earth
Until the end
Of your life
But I still hope
You come back
Someday.

I have the hope
That I will be happy
One day.
I always talk
In the echo
Of solitude
I do not deny.
I have experienced
The difference
When I have
Valid company.

I hope
That wherever
You are,
You remember
My love
And you wish
To see me,
Because
I feel the same way.

September 6, 1980

If You Were

If you were
The love I dreamt of,
I would fill you with kisses
As I did
With the one before.

If you were
The one I dream of,
I would make you my own
And to be honest,
I like you
But something is missing
That fulfills my emotions.

If you were
The love of my life,
Happiness
Would always be
A blessing.

March 8, 1978

Love In An Interval

Love in an interval
Is what you give me
In the dark.
As evening falls,
I remember your manners
And your love.

Love in an interval
Starts in the evening,
Goes through the night
And lasts until dawn.

Love in an interval
Is ours
So we do not hurt others.

If, unfortunately,
We see each other
In the daytime
With other company,
We pretend
Not to know each other
Because this is only
Love in an interval.

June 3, 1979

I Am Sorry

I am sorry.
That night
You left me,
Now I ask you,
Stay here with me,
And let us be more
Than just friends.

Let this night
Make us see
Everything afresh
As if we had just met.
That night
You showed interest
But you left
And I was saddened.

November 9, 1978

Our Love

At night,
When I look
At the dark skies,
I imagine myself
By your side
And I see you smile.
The same way it was
The night we met,
I loved
Your unforgettable smile.

Our love
Was brief
But beautiful.
There will not be
Another love
Like this again.

February 10, 1980

I Need You

Because I need you,
My days
Are centuries
And my nights
Are eternity.
Without you
My life
Is inconsequential,
My heart
Is like a burnt candle
And my feelings
Are not real.

The sky is not blue
Because I need you.
I need you
To change my mood.

November 20, 1979

Forever An Illusion

I fell in love
The first time we met
And though
You are not here,
I still care.

In dreams
I see you happy
Because of our love,
I see you smile,
You see me,
We embrace,
We kiss,
Satisfaction is seen.

I love you
Even if you
Do not return,
You are someone else's
And also
You belong to me.
I do not think
I know you,
But I feel
You are the love of my life.

In dreams, I see you,
I see you by my side
And in my fantasies
I am happy with you.

I wish for nothing more
Than to be with you.
My happiness is endless
Because you are
The love of my life
In the fantasy I live.

January 28, 1981

Where Are You?

Love,
Where are you?
I want to see you,
And be in your arms,
And kiss your lips.

Though distance
May be great
And time
May be unending,
Have no doubts
That I still love you.

People look at me
With sadness
As I walk
Through the streets
Aimlessly,
Hoping to find
The one
Who gives me
Encouragement.

Each time
I hear your name,
I ask myself,
Love,
Where are you?
I know
Wherever you may be,
You will remember me.

With you up to the end,
Until the time comes
For me to leave this life,
I ask,
Love,
Where are you?
Asking for your return.

September 21, 1980

Nostalgia

Nostalgia
Invaded my heart,
Reality stepped over
My dreams,
The weeping
From my eyes
Bathes my soul
In tears of pain
Over a love
That became a dream
And never will be true.

I love you,
I cannot deny it.
Of my life,
This is the most beautiful.
Being away
Doesn't help me
Forget you.
Days pass,
And months
And I still
Remember you.

The terrible nostalgia
Made me a prisoner,
You will never be mine,
I know.
Your soul is bound
To past memories
And that
Makes you suffer.

I have ruined
The dreams
That, with you
And for you,
I once had.
I wasted
All your love,
Before time
And now
That I do not have it,
Everything
Has collapsed.

Nostalgia
And sadness
Have formed
A valley of tears
In my troubled soul.
Melancholy
Seized my being
With no reason
Or warning.

December 30, 1979

Doubt

I dream you are here
Next to me,
And I feel complete,
I am happy
But I awake
And cannot find you.

Because of you,
I made castles,
Houses, in the air,
On the sea,
Nests of cotton
That vanish,
As I awake.

You and I,
Only one,
One soul in two bodies.
You are just a doubt,
You are an illusion
That sustains me
With natural beauty.

February 3, 1982

My Pleading

Listen
To the pleading
I ask,
Please,
I ask, I beg.

This pleading comes
From my love
For you.
Pleading of love,
Pleading of poverty,
Is what I feel
Without your warmth.

This is the pleading
That came
From my heart
When I think
What I would give
To have a bit
Of your love.

June 15, 1979

My Love For You

You ask me
What my love is for you.
I will tell you all it is,
It is something
Beautiful I feel
And it is happiness
When I see you.

It has no pride,
It's neither silent
Nor shameful,
If I want, I can say it
And let everyone know
That I love you
And I am happy.

It is a sigh,
A beautiful word,
A true smile,
A kiss
When you please,
And an embrace
When I feel defenseless.

It is like a rainy day
In a cabin
Well protected,
It is like
An afternoon in May
As the sun sets
Over the lake,
It is like a starry night
With the moon,
Luminous,
By the ocean side.

It has no dismissal
It is not a fling,
Not a dream,
Not insanity,
Simply it is love—
Has always been
And will forever be.

July 1, 1979

The Day

The day
You came to me,
I loved you.
The day you left,
I tried forgetting you,
I made you an idol
Since the day we met.

You left me
Something pleasant,
Now I think about you
As something
With no end.

When I met you,
You gave me memories,
And now that you leave,
You give me your oblivion,
But I cannot accept it
Without motives.

January 21, 1978

Tomorrow

I met you
In a park
One afternoon in April,
And by January
I lost you.
Each morning
I go back to that park
And sit
On the same bench,
Though many years
Have passed.

As always,
You said
You would return
Tomorrow,
But that tomorrow
Never arrived.
You thought
I would not be hurt
If you left
Without saying a word.

To say,
Tomorrow I will,
Is to make a promise
With no sense,
And you
Made me believe so.
It is I, who suffered
The consequences
Of your oblivion.

Today, like always,
I have come back
To the park
Of my memories.
I am surprised
To see you here,
I realize
I've come here
Out of habit.
I do not need you
Anymore,
It is all dead
And you have hopes.

Why are you back?
I was used
To being without you.
Remember
That the tomorrow
Of your promises,
Now will not come
From my part.
.

July 24, 1979

EVENTS

Days of festivities,
Days of celebration,
Days of remembrance,
Special places
And important days
Become events.

A Father

When you feel
The warmth
Of your child
In your arms,
Remember,
He will follow
In your steps.

As you see him
Grow up,
Laugh and cry,
He'll bring you pride.
As father
And friend,
You will see
In his eyes
The reflection
Of what you have lived.
His youth
Will remind you
Of your life,
And you will know
They are stories
Being repeated.

Give time,
Love and attention
To the children
You may have.
Treat them all
The same,

Remember,
It is more important
To give
Time than money.

When
He has made his home
And has an heir,
You will see
He followed
Your steps
And you are living
In each one of them.

April 2, 1979

That Party

At that party
You met me
And, not knowing
How I was,
You loved me.
I gave you wings
To fly
In other skies,
But as I saw you
Wanting to take me
With you,
I cut them off,
And irredeemably,
You stayed here
With me.

Since that party,
I cannot stay away
From you,
But I have not been sincere.
I failed to say
I was there for the fun
And I played
To seduce you.
Now
I regret it.
Yesterday
You were pleased.
Today, at times,
It is as if I do not exist.

At that party,
I was
The happiest woman,
Today,
I am the most unfortunate,
Because instead
Of you
Falling in love,
I am the one
In love with you.

November 10, 1979

Essence Of Innocence

The Lord sent you
From the heavens
To fill
The empty cradle
With your warmth
To cover the cold
Like no other can,
It had to be
Especially you.

I engendered you
With love
In the dreams
Of my life.
In the essence
Of innocence,
I so yearned for you.
You came
From nothing,
From some fairy tale
Or witchcraft.

You arrived
With the sweet
Innocence
In the enchantment
Of a kiss,
I did not know
What it was
But now
I believe it pure,
Full of tenderness.

One of many days
You came to me
And heaven
Lost an angel.
My suffering
Became such a joy
And I heard
Beautiful singing
When I heard
Your laughter.

My thoughts
Navigated
Through fantasies
And I imagined you
A thousand ways.
In that world
Everything
Was so still,
I heard only
The whispers
Of our voices
And the birds singing.
The echo
Of your laughter
And of your cries
Was strong
Among the mountains,
As strong
Within me
When you announced
Your arrival.

I saw you
For the first time.
You cried
Exasperated,
And a part of me
Went with you.
You belonged
To me,
You were mine.
In your soft skin
A hidden scent
Appeared,
It was the essence
Of innocence.

Your face,
Childish,
Beautiful
And tender,
Reflected
The sweetness
Of childhood.
My beautiful
Baby,
You were innocent
To pain and evil.
I cradle you softly
And never got tired
Of seeing you.
You were
A shower of joy,
You were
A white dove,
And my heart
Was your home.

My beautiful child,
You had peace.
Time passed
So quickly,
Your body
Was taking
A different form.
Your hair,
Long and black,
Was a toy
To the wind.
Your face
Was a unique image,
And at same time,
It was familiar.
Your peaceful face,
Your fragile body,
Reflected happiness,
It was a great
Feeling,
It was the essence
Of innocence.

I am your mother,
As a child,
I was your protector,
Now I want
To be your friend.
I wanted you
Always by my side,
Child, pure, kind,
With the essence
Of innocence
But love arrived
And takes you away.

Where
Was my child
With the essence
Of innocence
Of pure
Sentiments,
Nice, kind,
And always happy?

You played
With rag dolls
Innocently,
Now to satisfy
Your desires,
You look
For passion
In some manly arms.

The cruel time
Didn't listen
To my prayers.
Time passed
And your childhood
Was becoming
The charms
Of a woman.

Today,
Dressed in white,
You share
Your life
With a lover,
A romantic dreamer,
Just like you
And I feel proud
When I give you away
To him.

December 1, 1982

(To my grandmother)

On Mother's Day,
The good sentiments
Should be shown
And the happy moments
Must be remembered.

I hope that this day,
Your children
And grandchildren
Make you happy,
May every child
Give you love,
May you feel happy,
Never sad,
Though you are far
From me,
I want to let you know
That in spirit I am near.

April 7, 1978

St. Nick

On December 24,
At twelve midnight,
St. Nick arrives
In his swift sleigh
Loaded with toys.
December 24,
When children
Sleep impatiently,
Waiting
For the new dawn
They always remember.

St. Nick,
With his beard,
Long and white,
Is the children's delight,
He gives
Pure tenderness
From his good heart
And in exchange
He gets affection
And a thousand thanks.

The saints
Join him,
And they start a chant
Of happiness
And devotion
That turns laughter
Into tears
As he leaves.

As a Christmas gift,
I will ask God
And the world
That love,
Peace and liberty,
Prevail everywhere
So as Jesus
And St. Nick.

November 30, 1980

Fifteen Years

Turning fifteen years old
Was not easy,
It is when I felt
The saddest,
And it was all difficult.

Standing
In front of the mirror,
I saw the years
Fall upon me.
Old age got to me,
And I thought
The end was near.

It was conflictive,
The sadness
And the expectation,
The happiness
And the worries.
I realized,
It is either life or death,
And I chose to live.
Death arrives
Whenever it wants to.

A birthday
Is one more stage
Of a person's life
To reflect
And, at times, to accomplish
What we wished.

Fifteen years old
Happens only once,
But forever I keep
Those memories
In my heart

August 26, 1978

February 14

February 14,
Day for lovers.
I love you,
Is said
To everyone dear.
On Valentine's Day
It is said,
I will be with you
To the end.

With this carnation
I show you
That in my being
There is a distress
That no one can calm
Like you can
With your friendship.

Today we say
Many beautiful
Things,
And instead of smiling,
We cry
For those things,
As small,
That come from the heart.

February 14,
May love exist forever
Within the whole world.
This is for the true friend
And for the dreamers too.

February 9, 1979

Our Day

I hope
As you read
These simple letters,
Your heart is moved
As mine is
When I see you.

This special day
Belongs to us,
This Valentine's Day,
As the past ones
And the ones to come,
Are our celebration.

This date
Is to honor
Our love,
We celebrate
Friendship and love,
Between you and I
Is truth
And affection
As friends
And heated love
As lovers.

In life
Suffering is accepted
And happiness
Is seized
And I, sweetheart,
Am happy day by day.

Wait for me
In our castle
Of dreams.
It will not take long
To see the end
Of this beautiful night.
I will bring
My kisses and love
As a special gift.

February 12, 1980

Sweet Sixteen

Sweet sixteen,
You have become
A young woman
Of a society
That now starts
To acknowledge you
And they want
Your views
As a restless woman.

Sweet sixteen,
You feel like the queen
Of the world,
In your innocence,
You think
The world
Is in your hands
And the men
Are at your feet,
You see suitors
And Prince Charming
At your disposition.

Sweet sixteen,
No one is as sweet
As you,
Happiness is everything
For you.
Queen of youth,
Your laughter
Is naïve and free.

Sweet sixteen,
Enjoy.
This year
Is a special,
This is when women
Feel most excited.
Unexpected reactions
Are surpassed.
I know,
Because I, too,
Was once upon a time
A sweet sixteen.

June 19, 1980

Amid Smoke And Ashes

Between smoke
And ashes
Your memories
Disappear.
The words
Vanish in the air
Like the smoke
Of the cigarette.
Smoking,
And with a glass
In hand,
I remember you
Sweetly,
I cannot forget
The kisses
You gave me
So passionately.

I remember
The beautiful days
That I spent happy
By your side.
I daydreamt of you,
Knowing
You would never
Be totally mine.

It's autumn again,
And it is cloudy,
I remember you
Even more

As I see the leaves
On the ground
And I feel this cold air.
I do not know
If it's the memories,
The wine, or smoke,
But I'm tearing up.

I am alone
In the apartment
That we shared,
Once bright
And warm,
It is now silent
And darkened.

By the window,
I wish to see back,
I feel so far
From here
The music
Takes away
My thoughts,
The smoking is endless,
Time has gone by.

Evening is approaching,
And I have to go.
I waited so long,
And you did not arrive,
I cannot take the solitude,
So I left.

November 27, 1979

SURROUDINGS

The surroundings
Bring such inspiration
That is blurred
And intertwined
With love.

Springtime

Flowers are born,
Just as our love
Was born,
With water
Love and attention.
It is all more beautiful
When it is newly born
And everything
Seems better.

Springtime is
When winter leaves
Along with solitude,
Springtime is
When love arrives
And pain goes away.

On the fields
There is a new color
And a splendid sunlight
That I wish arrives already.

December 22, 1977

Flowers Of My Garden

I have many flowers
In my garden
That die
But come back
The next year.
They are flowers
From home
And wilderness
Planted
All over my courtyard.

Of these flowers
I choose the best,
Violets, carnations,
Chrysanthemums,
Roses, jasmines,
And hydrangeas,
Because these
Are the most fragrant.

Without forgetting
The wildflowers,
Mallows, poppies,
And tulips,
With their beauty
They are most reserved
For special places.

But no flower
In terms of fragrance
Or for being
Given away,
Are like daisies,
Gladioli, lilies,
Or even sunflowers,
But among all,
These are the best.

May 21, 1979

A Withered Rose

A withered rose
Is only unhappiness
For you
And for me
With nothing to say.

It was a red rose
That lost its leaves
With time
And the treatment given.

But it is not necessary
To kill a rose
To know
You love me
Because you show me
And I consider it.

December 22, 1977

Under The Rain

Under the rain
I cry of sadness,
It is the misery
You give this heart.

Under the rain
Hard I weep
Because you
Are not attentive
To my love.
In torments
Of my pain
I console my love.

Under the rain
I walk on dark streets
Guided
By the lantern
On the corner.

May 25, 1979

Shelter

If time
And distance
Meant nothing,
I would be in your arms
Kissing you
Like in past life.

Your heart and bed
Are the best shelters
I have found
For my failed love.

You are a cave
For security,
Shelter me
In your heart
And make me feel
Protected
Because my heart
Loves you.

I want a heart
Sentimental,
Not a heart
That beats just to live,
That is why you are
The special shelter
That is only for me.

March 13, 1981

Moon

Moon,
From the skies above
With the radiance
You have,
Shine on my soul,
Shine on my heart.

Moon,
Bright Silver Star,
Shine on me.
Infinite space
Is for the dreamers
But before you
There is no past
Or future
Only a beautiful
Present tense.

Beautiful light,
Shine each night
By my window.
Moon
That seems so high
And beautiful
Like the stars,
Help me reach
What I dream
For me
And those around me.

July 23, 1980

A Bird

A bird
Is like the soul
That roams
In different directions
And different hearts.

A bird
Is like the spirit
That crosses
Through towns
And passes over
Problems.

A bird
Is like a person,
Free
Like the wind
And fiery
In its thinking.

A bird
Roams freely,
A person
Walks on earth slowly.

Sometimes
We feel free
Like a bird
And sometimes
We feel restricted
Like a prisoner.

May 17, 1979

Roses

Think of a woman
As a flower
When you see
A rosebush
As some names
Are hard to forget,
And Rose
Is one of them,
It is a color,
A flower,
And a name.

Often
For a special occasion
Roses are given,
Be they are orange,
White, yellow,
Pink, or red,
To a lover or friend.

The roses
Of my rosebush,
Soft and exquisite,
Have a delicate scent,
And aroma
For lovers.

That is why I say
That the roses,
Beautiful flowers,
Carry romance
In their silky petals,
Taste and pleasure
Is within
Everyone's reach.

June 20, 1979

Autumn Sentiments

Leaves fall off
The trees
And the red roses
Die out.

I feel like a child
Walking alone
On the roads,
It is windy and cold
And my heart
Feels empty.

Autumn,
On the verge of winter,
Summer leaves
And everything seems
To have been done
In vain.

December 22, 1977

Bird In Freedom

Little bird,
You, that, go
Through every path,
Tell me
Where is it better.

You foresee destiny,
I am tired
Of my insanity,
And now
I want to fly
Just like you.

Bird
Of all colors,
You bring joy
With your songs
Each day,
Each spring
Now go and tell me
Where the sun is shining.

Bird in freedom,
I want to be free
Like you.

August 22, 1978

REMEMBRANCE

The history
And cultures mixed
Are enlivened
By traditions
Of past living
That are remembered
With pleasure
And yearning.

There must be
Remembrance
Onward.
Our steps,
Our actions,
Our words,
Must show
Pride and respect
For where we come from
And for the new culture
That came to be
So new generations
Will succeed.

Yearning

I am far
From my dear
Homeland.
Long is the distance
And the years
That separates me
From my country
But even so,
I still miss
My beloved Mexico.

I miss seeing
The innocent
Children
Playing in the streets
And making
Of any space
A field for their games.
And the demure
Girls
And daring
Boys,
The women
With their shawls
Talking
With their neighbors,
And the men
With their straw hats
Sharing laughs
And drinks
On the corner.

I miss
The parks,
Places of reunion
To celebrate,
Any excuse
To have music
And dancing.
I miss those nights
Where the couples
On the balconies
Had a romantic
Serenade.

My country
Of incomparable
Name,
Any simple street
Is a model worthily
For a painting.
The streets
At dawn
Have the scent
Of clay
And wet dirt,
Of poverty
And peace
With the coffee
Mixed in.

In the houses
Of adobe
And cardboard,
Poverty abounds,
But love
Is not missing.
Again, I want

To drink coffee
From a clay cup
And eat tacos
With beans
And peppers.
Everything
In memory
Looks prettier
And tastes
More delicious.

In your churches,
Cathedrals
And temples,
I want to ask for help
For all neighbors.
I wish to return
To the country
Of culture
And history,
Prosperity
And tradition.
I wish to go back
To the innocent way
I saw it
When I was young
And laughed freely.

May 25, 1980

Cinco De Mayo

Mexico,
Cinco de Mayo.
Many patriots
Gave their lives
In that revolution
So that today we all
Could preserve
Liberty and union.

Cinco de Mayo,
Unforgettable date,
The French
Our land invaded
But we proudly
Showed our
Bravery
And strength.

Mexico,
You bravely
Answered
To fight
The foreigners.
Your soldiers gave much
With no weapons
For protection.
Mexico,
You neither flinched
Nor stopped.
Your soldiers
Fought with no rest.

México,
Proud I am of you,
For your past
And your future.

April 23, 1979

My Homeland

I miss you,
And I respect you
More each day.
Over
Your beautiful
Fields
I want to spread
My tears
And make them
Bloom
At each step
I give.
In your fertile land
I want to be buried.

Your children
Are brave men,
Proud and dignified,
And your women
Are of unequal beauty.

You are shelter
For those
Who come to you,
You are the heart
Of the universe,
You are a big
And beautiful country,
In your airs
You breathed
Free and happy
Atmosphere.

My beautiful
Homeland,
You are glorious
Because you have
The Virgin Mary
In your map.
Hospitality,
Justice and freedom
Do not cease here.

Wherever
I may be
In the world,
I remember you
With love,
Admiration
And pride.

January 5, 1981

REFLECTIONS

Knowing yourself
Is to reflect.
We need to reflect
On what we've lived
To accept the facts
And be at peace.
We need to reflect
To make changes
And plan
A better life.

Life And Death

Life
Is not
How we plan it.
One hopes
For the best,
For happiness
And harmony,
But one always finds
Solitude
On that day.

It is believed
That death
Is the solution
With no questions
Or answers
But those
Who remain alive
Carry that load
In their conscience.

Occasionally,
And for our disconcert,
Death takes
The innocent
And good beings
And leaves
The wicked
And selfish here.

Life is
Only an episode,
And death is
A transition
Where
We all become
As one,
Nothing else matters
But the soul.

June 30, 1979

Final Loss

There's mourn
In my soul,
I have lost
My innocence,
My love,
And my peace.
My body
Is covered
In a black dress
And a dark veil
Covers my face
So no one can see
The pain
I live with.

I lost my child,
Forever
She closed
Her eyes,
The eyes
Of a restless
And mischievous
Six-year-old.

Lord,
Forgive me
For sending
Her away
With the hopes
She would have
A better life
But the keeper
Denied her warmth,
Bread and peace.
Instead,
By accident,
She found death
In her own games.

Lord,
Take her
To your kingdom
In heaven.
Protect her
With your angels
As she has suffered enough.

July 1, 1980

I Am Nothing

I feel lonely
Being surrounded
By people,
I feel I am nothing,
Though
They believe me
To be smart,
Sometimes I feel
No one loves me,
They are not interested,
They do not worry,
But they are
Always at my watch.

I feel lonely,
I feel
Nostalgic and sad
Being among
So many happy faces,
I believe myself
To be in poverty
But I am on a pedestal.

I feel I am trash
Because I do not give
Or receive tenderness,
I feel like this,
Very little,
Though I have it all.
I feel I am nothing,

Sometimes
I feel forgotten,
And I am equal
To everyone.
But all I say,
I feel it
Profoundly.

If anyone were to listen
When I speak,
If anyone
Would offer
Their support,
What joy
That would bring.

December 10, 1979

Youth

What is childhood?
What is youth?
Is it a long time
That seems short
Because it goes by
Flying,
Leaving only
Streaks and prints?

Might youth be
A season
In which to enjoy
Many things?
A season
Of wishes
And dreams
Of friends
And lovers,
Success
And wealth,
But never of poverty,
Defeats
Or failures?

As the years pass,
We leave our
Youth behind.
We then ask,
What is old age?
Is it a short time
That seems long,
Filled with experiences,
Memories,
And worries
Over anything
Minimal?

In old age,
We teach
The lessons
Learned of life
So youngsters
Do not fail
The same way
We have
But they live,
Fail, fall,
And learn
Exactly the same way
We did.

But,
Let us not get ahead,
Let us live
Our youth,
Though our faces
Show it has gone by,
Let us show everyone
That neither childhood
Nor youth
Has gone
From our hearts.

June 17, 1979

Craziness

Craziness.
There are people
Worse than me,
But in my burdens,
I think to be
The only one
In the world
Who suffers.
If some sad thing
Happens,
Unpleasant,
Or some failure,
I want to die.
I feel frustrated,
Ashamed of myself
For not being perfect
As I see others.

I love silence,
I love darkness,
I love to be alone
To be able to think
And put my thoughts
In order.
I want to cry,
I feel the desire
To scream,
Relieve my pain,
Hurt the universe—
Just as I feel too.

I wish to rise
To infinity,
Without being
Or having
Anyone's dominion.
I know
If I were to cry,
I would vent my soul,
My eyes
Would reflect peace,
Sorrow and doubt
Would leave
That I feel
Is killing me
But I cannot do so,
There's no real
Reason for this
And I would be judged
As crazy.

I am set aside,
I see others
With their obvious
Problems
Live happy,
I do not belong
To anyone,
I do not fit in
Anywhere,
I feel so alone
And those
Who do not know me,
Say I am likable
But for those
Who know me,
I am disposable.

How I wish
To sleep
And never wake up,
I wish
To close my eyes
To eternity,
Where no one
Would disturb
My thoughts,
I wish to be me
And not the reflection
Of who created me.

Appearances
Are all I have left
To face the world.
I wish
To close my eyes
And to open them
Never again,
The nostalgia
I feel
Would soon
Be forgotten,
I wish to travel
To a world
Of dreams
Where I am
The only one.

It is only craziness
That envelops
My mind
On my lonely
Sad days.
We all have
Problems,
Weaknesses and flaws,
We all have
Disabilities,
Hidden or visible,
Slight or strong,
We all have issues,
Mental or physical,
That need
To be uncovered,
To help ourselves
And others
But we only see
The flaws
Of those
In front of us.

Help me, Lord,
Survive
This ungrateful
World,
Fear nothing
And to obey
Your commands.
Help me
Not feel inferior,
Because we all
Should be equal
In life
If we are all the same
When life ends.

April 25, 1980

Tears, Tears

We are born crying,
And we die crying.

Tears, tears,
From sadness
Or pain,
On all our faces
Roll down.

Tears, tears,
Are from anguish,
Jealousy, joy
Or a goodbye,
A new beginning
Or for a loved one.

Tears, tears,
From surprises,
Good or bad,
For a kiss,
For a wish
Not accomplished,
For a return,
Always roll down.

Crying we are born
And crying we leave
And while we are here,
Always will there be
Tears, tears.

May 26, 1979

Lamentations

I lament the day
I put my writings
In strangers' hands.
I let them go
Without thinking
What would happen next.

Only laments
Are left,
I lost my writings
And lamentations
And regrets
Are only left.

What I write
Is part of me,
Those writings
Are my greatest
Treasure,
I believe
Are now lost,
I do not know what to do.

With laments
And regrets I live,
But I often ask God
This not be the case.
Those writings
Were my thoughts
And my past.

I pray to God
I would have
My treasure
In my hands again.
If only
I can have them,
I will lend them
Never again.

September 1, 1979

Time

I keep
My sorrows
In memories
Of yesterday
And I have
My hopes
In a probable
Tomorrow
When there will be
Less time
To say and think
What we want to deny.

Tomorrow
Is a time
That arrives sooner
Than expected.
Emotions are felt
In its given time,
And sometimes
There is no need
To say it
To show them.
There is time
To feel emotions
In their due time.

I will say, Yes,
To everything
I have dreamt.
There will be time
To be
What I wanted to be
Until it is time to die.

May 23, 1979

Lies

We all tell
Some lies,
From my part,
I know
I have lied enough
But my lies
Are not frequent
Or serious.

To tell a lie
Is to offer a hand
To those who ask,
But when they
Get into trouble,
No one cares,
Conditions come
Or the help received
Is limited.

I have asked
For help
And it was denied.
So close
To the people
But I have felt forgotten.
People tell me
They love me,
But that love
Hasn't been
Shown to me.

I do not like lies,
I am honest
And direct,
Though I try
Not to offend,
I prefer it this way
Than to fall
In the trap
Of continuous lies.

Let us forgive
The lies
And be honest.
In love,
Joy has little meaning
If not enjoyed
In time.

July 9, 1979

A Vagabond

A vagabond,
Walks alone
And sad
Through the world,
Carries
Misfortunes
In his heart
Thinking
What could be
Tomorrow
And afterward.

A vagabond
Destroys his soul
And causes pity
And shame.
He cries
And gets discouraged
By the insults
That some give
Without measure.

But someday
Happiness
Will arrive
To his heart
With new dreams,
Hopes and life.

There are those
Who have a conscience
And lend a hand
To lift up
A neighbor
And friend.

February 17, 1978

Time Goes By

Time goes by,
It goes by
Like birds flying,
It goes by unobserved
Between our hands.

Time goes by,
It runs fast and free
Like the wind
Leaving only memories.

Time moves,
Neither stops
Nor turns back.
It seems
Just like yesterday
When I came
Into this world
But so many years
Have passed
From that one minute.

Time
Has brought me
Joy and suffering,
Experiences
And disillusion,
Disappointments
And hopes
And I accepted it all.

Today we say,
Tomorrow
I will do
Such-and-such,
Since I did not
Have time today.
We plan things,
But in time
Nothing
Comes out right
Because time
Is time.

Time fixes
Everything
And gives the answer.
But time goes by
And we go with it,
And in time
We do nothing,
For time
Is just that,
Time.

July 9, 1979

My Luck

I curse my luck.
I feel
Very unfortunate
And I ask myself
If I have
A guardian angel
Like everyone else.
And the answer
Comes by itself:
No!

In other instances,
I bless my luck
And I am thankful
To God
For sending me
Such happiness.

I get to thinking,
How bleak
Is my luck!
But after
Meditating
On what happened,
I realize
If something is wrong,
It is only
Because of me.

Luck
Does not arrive
By itself,
It is part of destiny
That is already
Written,
And it is part
Of what we do,
The sacrifices made,
To break down barriers
And do what we can.

October 23, 1979

Aspiration

Someday
I will be
Where I want to be,
Someday
I will be
What I really
Want to be,
Someday
I will be
With whomever I want,
On land
Or at sea,
But together
Forevermore.

Someday
My dreams
Will be fulfilled,
And I will ask
Nothing from anyone,
Someday
Heaven
Will be all mine,
Nothing
Will be foreign
Or unknown.

Someday
My aspirations
Will be satisfied,
But perhaps
That day
Will be the end
Of my life.

April 5, 1981

DEDICATIONS

Some people
Make a bigger impression
Than others,
Some people
Say the right things
At the right time,
Some people
Lift you up,
Some people's presence
Makes all the difference.

Your Voice

Your mysterious voice
Intrigues me
And wish to know you.
In the distance
Your voice
Sounds sensitive,
Kind and patient.

I like your soft voice
Though unknown,
I find it
Seductive and friendly.
Your voice,
A bit sensual,
Somewhat romantic,
Provokes my senses
And to you
I feel attracted.

Your voice is unique,
Your voice is special,
It is melodious
And attractive,
It captures
My total attention,
It makes me dream,
And makes me think
And I want always
To listen more of it.

June 10, 1980

My Friend

I call you
My friend
Because you witness
My sorrows
And joys,
You come to me
When I need you,
You are next to me
Day by day
And you bring relief
To my sadness
With words
Of tender affection.

My friend,
You are my confidant,
I love you
Like a brother,
You are never far
And are always
At my care.

My friend,
Count on me
On issues
Of friendship
Or affairs,
You showed me
My self-worth
And I have given you
My friendship.

You are
My friend,
My dear friend,
You make me
Rectify
The mistakes
Of my life.
My friend,
Thank you
For being this way,
For being patient
And giving me
Hope
That everything
Will get better.

March 10, 1980

#

If time
Could stand still,
I would not be apart
From you,
If the wind
Could be seen,
I could see clearly
Everything.

The wind
And the sea
Are to be admired,
Time
And you
Are like eternal
Youth.
Close to you,
I rather not know
Anything
So I will not suffer.

You,
Who gives me
The forbidden love,
You,
Who burns me
With that hidden fire,
Make time
Be stopped
So I can stay
With you.
Make the wind
Be gone
So I will not be cold.
With you
I forget everything,
I just live my life.

May 29, 1979

Greetings

A farewell
Is always sad
But greetings
Are always happy.
You left one place
To arrive
At another forever.

You will be happy
Over there,
I know,
We will miss you,
I am sure.
They are waiting
For you
With open arms,
And here,
We close ours
As we say in silence
See you soon,
Not a good bye.

Materials
I do not give,
For they do not last,
Words
Go with the wind,
Feelings,
With distance
And time,
Are forgotten.

I wish you happiness
And a long life
And may God
Bless you
Where you are.
A humble thought
I give you
And I hope as you read,
You remember
We miss you.

Do not feel obligated
To offer
Your gratitude,
It is the affection
You make us feel
That, with this thought,
I give thanks
For all
You did for me.

June 22, 1980

To My Mother

I was a seed
In your womb,
Fruit,
That with simplicity
You gave birth,
I am a branch
Of your roots
Watered
With your tears,
But you cared for me
With love
And tenderness.

Mother,
Thank you
For giving me life,
For overcoming
Poverty
To care of me
At every moment,
You made
Of every sacrifice
A daily routine,
You are a woman
Of your home
And for your children,
You are the beat
Of my conscience,
And a good example
To follow.

Forgive
My bad behavior
And give me
Your blessing.
Though I live in peace,
I know things
Could have been better.

May 9, 1980

Graduation

The end of one phase
And the beginning
Of another,
Graduations divide
The known of yesterday
To the expectations
And mysteries
Of tomorrow.

The diploma says,
Behind remains
Childhood, safety
And protection
Of the system.
A paper tells me
I fulfilled
The requirements
Although I wasn't,
A very good student
Or apprentice
But the paper,
Opens up new paths.

Some friends
Have their future
Planned out
And remain content,
And I, I wasn't sure
How to begin,
Or in what setting,
But writing
Was my dream.

Time for goodbyes
To my friends,
Hugs
Of good wishes,
Promises
Of keeping in contact,
Gladness and smiles
For achieving
The goal
And sadness for all
That is left behind.

The book
Of memories
Tells me
I was friends
With so many people.
They all said
I should not change
Because my frankness
Was unique
And special.
The promises
Of those days
Remain forever written
But never became true.
Each one
Took a path
To their liking
And need.

December 30, 1982

www.ingramcontent.com/pod-product-compliance
Lightning Source LLC
LaVergne TN
LVHW011712060526
838200LV00051B/2878